THAI FORMS

NX 5

THAI FORMS

THAI FORMS

text by Jean-Michel Beurdeley
photos by Hans Hinz

WEATHERHILL
New York & Tokyo

Frontispiece: detail of a curtain at the National Theatre, Bangkok. The design shows a traditional Thai motif.

This book was originally published in French in 1979 by Office du Livre, Fribourg, Switzerland, under the title *Thaïlande des formes.*
English translation by Alison Martin

First English edition, 1980

Published by John Weatherhill, Inc., of New York and Tokyo, with editorial offices at 7-6-13 Roppongi, Minato-ku, Tokyo, Japan. Copyright © 1980 by Office du Livre, Fribourg, Switzerland; all rights reserved. Printed in Spain and first published in Japan.

Library of Congress Cataloging in Publication Data:
Beurdeley, Jean-Michel / Thai forms. / Translation of Thailande des Formes. / 1. Folk art – Thailand. / 2. Thailand – Popular culture. / 3. Form (Aesthetics) / I. Hinz, Hans. / II. Title. / NX578.7.A1B4813 / 745.09593 / 79-28518 / ISBN 0-8348-0150-7

Thai Forms

This study of the formal beauty of everyday objects in Thailand does not claim to be an ethnological work, for the scientific approach lies outside our province. We have not, however, restricted ourselves to a description of the plastic beauty of these objects, as this might impose on them an aesthetic motive that was never intended. Our aim, in fact, is to show articles that have been designed for a special purpose and constructed from materials strictly suited to that purpose. Beauty is born out of this harmonious relationship between use, shape and material.

The field of investigation in Thailand was immense, ranging from objects used in Buddhist religious services to simple household utensils, with a selection of agricultural implements, musical instruments, toys and even certain architectural features in between, as well as a few selected items from the Siamese court. The choice was not easy. Moreover, it is almost impossible to establish clear dividing lines between folk art, decorative art and art in general. If we sometimes go beyond our aim and show the hands of a dancer, for example, which open like an exotic flower, this is to emphasize the connection between the living and the plastic forms of the most familiar objects.

Some of these articles are still in use, while others have become obsolete. As observers from a different culture, it was perhaps easier for us to look at them with a discerning eye: the sickle used by Siamese peasants in the nineteenth century resembles a sculpture by Arp – or perhaps it is rather the sculpture that resembles the sickle; in the theatre, a mask is used not only for disguising reality but also as an aid to the creation of a whole world of imaginings and feelings; and the fighting cock's cage with its slender willow bars, crossed with twisted cord, is astonishingly perfect in its rustic construction. Whatever their appearance and purpose and to whatever level of life these objects belong, they are all characteristically Thai, reflecting Thai traditions and mentality.

The reader will not, we trust, object that we have been too free in our choice. We have tried to seek out expressions of an art that still exists, although it is threatened more and more each day. We have not attempted to provide a catalogue, not wishing to write an encyclopaedic work any more than a scientific one. We have been led solely by our love for this country.

The following guide, which is more of a narrative than an analysis, has been wonderfully illustrated by Hans Hinz. Sharing enthusiasm, he has captured all the subtleties of this complex civilization with his magic lens, and with objective images, he has managed to reconstitute all Thailand's singularity and charm.

Art is nothing other than
the creation of forms.
Goethe

If one tries to enumerate the arts, it is very difficult to know where to stop. Should make-up, for example, the art of beautifying the body, be included? May not tattooing, flower arranging and cooking also be regarded as art forms? There are many objects that are attractive and useful, but where can we place dividing lines between all the different concepts? 'Art is nothing other than the creation of forms,' said Goethe. But surely it is necessary to complete this definition by adding to the notion of beauty those of pleasure, taste, love and aural perception as Epicure did before us. A few decades ago, the New York Customs refused to acknowledge a sculpture by Brancusi, *Bird in Flight,* as a work of art, which meant that it was not exempt from duty. However, the purchaser finally won his case by claiming that it 'could only be used for purely decorative purposes and not utilitarian ones'. Luckily this conception of art is peculiar only to customs services. Who nowadays would be so bold as to deny that objects that combine utility with aesthetic qualities are works of art?

It was only in the middle of the last century that Europeans really began to show an interest in the products of the skilled craftsman. The term 'folklore' was invented in 1846 by W. J. Thoms in *Atheneum.* The Crystal Palace Exhibition held in London in 1851 was particularly revealing in this context. It was followed in 1852 by the founding of the Victoria and Albert Museum, where one entire section was devoted to the 'applied' arts. During the same year oriental goods shops appeared in Regent Street. At this time William Morris, vanquisher of Victorian taste, put forward new artistic theories and reinstated the artisan as he who creates with his own hands.

In France, the Universal Exhibition of 1867 brought to the notice of the public the skilled crafts that had grown out of various traditions in exotic countries. Among other things, model boats given to Napoleon III by the King of Siam and Siamese fishing tackle excited public admiration. Today, it is not merely the attraction of the exotic, the curiosity that a disappearing culture stimulates, or the fascination of the unusual or the peculiar that arouses interest in folk arts and crafts: it is rather the charm of the rustic materials and the simplicity of forms.

Those Europeans who travelled to Siam in the seventeenth and eighteenth centuries did not even bother to describe Siamese handicrafts. They were principally impressed by the luxury of the court. 'Never had they seen so much gold all in one place,' exclaimed Father Bouvet enthusiastically. Nicolas Gervaise, travelling to Siam in 1688, was granted the privilege of visiting the King's stores where he saw, 'Urns, piled on top of one another right up to the roof and full of *tical* (coins) ... to all the hidden treasures must be added those which may be seen by everyone – several sets of crockery in massive gold ... the countless diamonds and precious stones that embellish His Majesty's clothes and his horses' and elephants' harnesses; some rubies stand out among others because of their prodigious size ...' Father Bouvet, sent to Siam in 1685 to convert King Pra Narai to Christianity, describes the large gold and silver statues 'embellished with different gems', and 'the gilt roofs of the pagodas'. He deplores the fact that 'the Siamese are more magnificent in their temples than our Christians are in theirs'.

Father Bouvet may have been dazzled by the riches of the capital but another Frenchman, La Loubère, who accompanied the Embassy in 1687, appears to have been much less impressed. Steeped in traditional prejudice, he disposed of the works of the Siamese painters with one scornful glance. 'They imagine,' he wrote, 'flowers, birds and other animals that never existed. They sometimes place people in impossible positions, and the secret lies in giving all this a semblance of effortlessness which makes it appear natural.' And in conclusion La Loubère states that, the medium of oil being unknown to the Siamese, they must be 'poor painters'.

Another famous traveller, the ineffable Abbé de Choisy, who volunteered to go and convert the Siamese, shares this opinion. This strange ecclesiastic, known for his perverse tastes – he liked to dress up as a woman and did not attempt to hide his passion for showy dressing-gowns and embroidered corsets – was nonetheless erudite and a man of parts. Consequently he was entrusted with the task of choosing presents for Louis XIV. The *Memorial of the Presents from the King of Siam to the King of France* (1686) tells of much lacquer and porcelain, many caskets and fabrics from China, Japan and the Indies, but there is very little mention of local products. Among the latter there

was 'a three-tier filigree-gold vessel in which the letter for the King of France was carried'. La Loubère, who was very critical of Siamese art, regarded these filigree works as 'the most elegant in the world'. A drinking vessel of embossed gold decorated with precious stones, similar to these receptacles, was found at Wat Ratchaburana of Ayuthya. On 18 October 1685, when the Siamese king appeared at the window of the audience chamber (for he always had to be placed higher than the others at the ceremony), he was presented with the letter brought by the French ambassador in another similar vessel to which a handle had been fixed. There is also an allusion in the *Memorial* to a ewer of *tambacq* (an alloy of gold and copper), 'with a saucer for washing the hands, which had been made in Siam in the manner of that country' and 'two canons of beaten metal ornamented with silver, on mounts also ornamented with silver, made in Siam'. This list of the presents brought to Versailles by the Siamese ambassadors also includes 'a silk folding screen, decorated with birds and flowers standing out in relief on a blue background, made in Siam'.

It must be acknowledged that many more pieces of ceramics and other rarities from China and Japan than from Siam figure in these lists. In the seventeenth and eighteenth centuries Europeans looked on Siamese receptacles as 'vulgar and cheap,' whereas in the sixteenth century the more discerning Japanese art lovers sought out the deep soft-green celadons of Sawankhalok for the tea ceremony; no less did they value the stoneware of Sukhothai, the restrained colouring and slight irregularities of which demonstrate that it is the authentic work of skilled craftsmen. The Thai people themselves were convinced that the celadons changed colour if they came into contact with poisoned food. It was customary to attribute to this stone substance all sorts of magical qualities and to mix ground fragments of it with medicines or potions.

Ceramic art, which is more than 4000 years old, was making rapid progress towards the end of the thirteenth century and the beginning of the fourteenth when a Thai king (son of the founder of the Kingdom of Sukhothai), Rāma Khāmhèng (Rama the Strong), sent for more than 300 potters from China, the country from which the Thais originated. According to tradition the potters were installed in North Thailand, where they built several kilns in the region of Sukhothai, the old capital, and near Si Sacchanalai. Their products were exported to all the South-east Asian countries as far as the Philippines, and to Japan. At the Sukhothai digs, enormous jars, used to hold the ashes of the dead, were discovered. They had been previously 'destroyed' or perforated in order that they should not be used for any other purpose. Apart from ashes these jars contained mirrors, scissors, combs and all kinds of articles that had belonged to the deceased. Even today some village dwellers break the necks of old jars, so that the trapped spirits may escape and seek refuge elsewhere.

The ceramic tradition still prevails in Thailand, particularly that of stoneware with bold well-balanced shapes, corresponding to modern art criteria. Some of these pieces of stoneware were inspired by metalwork from India or ceramics from China, while others are purely Thai in origin, such as the pots used for cooking rice. The techniques, developed over centuries by the Thai villagers, are unfortunately now being threatened by soulless mass production. The same applies to the art of lacquerwork, which is relatively recent (having probably started around the sixteenth century) and which also bears witness to the manual and technical skill of the Thai craftsman. Although the repertoire of shapes and designs actually originated from the iconographical traditions of India, the perfect construction, the balance achieved between gold and black colouring, and the elegance of the mother-of-pearl inlays

may all be attributed to the taste of the Thai people.

Europeans of the eighteenth century were unaware of what we have tried to point out in this book, namely the aesthetic qualities of traditional objects, developed during the course of time by generations of anonymous artisans, most of them peasants, who, profiting from the lull during the dry season when the rice has been gathered, devoted themselves to their crafts. Exerting all their creative skill, they would make thousands of small ingenious articles, very often of exquisite taste: tiny dolls, coconut ladles, trays, fans. It was generally the men who made the baskets, straw hats and mattings, the women limiting themselves to weaving. The children helped with the work, as they still do today, and in this way traditions are perpetuated. Some villages specialize in the production of parasols, others in tiles or lacquerwork. These domestic crafts, intended for local use, are accompanied by numerous secondary activities connected with religious festivals and other celebrations: the art of wrapping things up, of tying knots, of presenting confectionary, of making banners and small bamboo or paper mobiles — fragile objects made from inexpensive materials, yet they add an incomparable grace to food offerings presented in the temple or on the family altar.

Flowers naturally play an important part in all these festivals and ceremonies. Abundant, varied and of a strange beauty, flowers are extremely suitable for impromptu decorations. Arranging such flowers may well be called an art. It is an art of an essentially feminine nature that was practised above all at the court. There are several instances of flower arranging mentioned in the *History of Nāng Nophāmat*, which was written more than 600 years ago, shortly after the invention of the Thai alphabet during the reign of Rāma Khāmhèng (1279–1316). Nāng Nophāmat describes the royal ceremonies, mentioning among others the festival of *Loï Kratong,* which takes place in November at full moon, to ask pardon of the water spirits for having soiled their domain. This is a popular festival, for not only are the king and leading citizens invited, but also the peasants and artisans. Everyone goes to the edge of the *klongs* and rivers to witness the enchanting vision of countless lanterns, with the most unexpected shapes and decorations, sailing on the water in a silver shimmer cast by the light of the moon. On this occasion the ladies of the court compete with each other in a test of taste and imagination. They construct vessels to carry offerings – these may consist of just a simple rice cake – which they build from flowers and petals, fashioned into harmonious translucent shapes and lighted from the inside. These floating master-pieces are presented to the king and then used to pay homage to Buddha, or more precisely to his footprints, on the bank of the River Nammada. Chinese lanterns shine everywhere; songs intermingle, punctuated at intervals with joyful blasts of fireworks. Nāng Nophāmat himself created an immense lotus-blossom from different coloured petals, topped with a minute bird, carved from the flesh of a piece of fruit. Charmed, the king decreed that in future this would be the model for all festival lanterns. It can still be seen today, in barely modified form.

Nāng Nophāmat also describes two-tier betel cups, elaborately decorated with flowers, that the king would offer to his visitors during audiences.

The names of queens are given to certain styles of floral arrangement at which they seem to have excelled – *Tani,* for instance, who was a member of the famous Bunnag family and wife of Rāma I (1782–1809). During the reign of Rāma V Chulalongkorn (1868–1910), the art of flower arranging progressed. The interest shown by the King encouraged the ladies of the court to introduce innovations, without however discarding the old techniques. Queen Saowabha Phongari, mother of

Rāma VI, created the models for garlands that were adapted for various different social and religious functions and used in the temple, the palace and on the family altar. Warakhananand, a lady of the palace, also made a reputation in this field.

Nowadays floral art is no longer the prerogative of the court and aristocracy. It is practised everywhere, in the street, on steps where everyone may supply themselves according to the requirements of the occasion. However, most of the bouquets that we photographed had been ordered from the court suppliers.

In addition to their decorative quality, flowers and trees have a symbolic value which may vary as time goes by. *Rak* flowers *(Calotropis gigantea)* were once used at cremations; today they are plaited in garlands for bridal couples. The *kluey tani* is a kind of banana-palm, the leaves of which are used as wrapping or to make cups. It is never planted near houses, because it is said to be inhabited by a female spirit or *phi,* the lovers' mediator. If you cut a root from this tree and give it a human form, the *phi* will haunt your dreams; no one should make so bold as to declare his love to a girl without asking the spirit's permission first. *Nang yaem (Cleredendron fragrans),* which means 'to half-open', appears often in the erotic literature of the country. When it grows old it is said to turn into a *phi,* which then disturbs the life of the household.

Apropos of *phis* it should be added that the Siamese have never lost their ancestral beliefs in animate spirits. They remain convinced that spirits of varying degrees of evil roam around them and that these spirits must be given a great deal of attention and a great number of offerings in order to render them harmless. In every house there is a small altar with ancestral relics on it to which the family makes offerings every day, while burning incense and invoking the spirits. The household gods play a prophylactic role: they prevent evil spirits from entering the house. Placed at the entrance to the garden, the household gods occupy a miniature house, standing on a pillar, that is liberally bedecked with flowers, incense sticks and food offerings.

The imagination of the Siamese craftsmen can be seen at work everywhere. Kite-flying, for example, which in Thailand is not only a distraction but an actual sport, has inspired some real master-pieces. Shapes – birds, flowers and mythical animals – and colours are rarely repeated. There are men's kites and women's kites, the former clearly being larger and armed with a piece of bamboo that is sharpened into a blade intended to cut the adversary's cord. From February to April, competitions take place between two opposing camps near the Bangkok Royal Palace. It is wonderful to see these colourful shapes, skilfully handled by the team members, as they flutter against the spring sky. At the beginning of the game the intent spectators lay bets. The winner is he who succeeds in bringing the largest number of kites into his own camp. In the eighteenth century, during the war between Siam and Burma, kites were used as missiles. They were lighted and directed over the enemy positions in the hope of setting them on fire.

The Thais have a keen taste for music. It accompanies them not only in their leisure activities but on all occasions. Music is played at the Palace, in the towns and in the most primitive rural communities. For several years now the official authorities have been trying to collect and preserve all the old traditional elements – melodies, songs and instruments. This rescue work is due largely to Princes Damrong Rājanubhab and Nariśra-Nuvattivariśa, who have devoted a great deal of their expertise towards it. Instruments were hand-made with great skill, and although some were borrowed from southern China and India, most of them are genuinely and characteristically Thai. Rather primitive at first, they were given onomatopœic names recalling the sounds they made. In due course they evolved, while still retaining their original qualities.

All Thai orchestras have two types of instruments: wind and, by far the most numerous, percussion. The *ránāt ayk* (Pl. 32), for example, consists of a long keyboard on a wooden stand that also serves as a sound box. This elongated and slightly concave instrument is reminiscent of the Thai river boats. The current model of the *ránāt ayk* has about twenty keys that are usually made from two different kinds of bamboo. As Thai music developed, this was judged to be an insufficient number, and a new instrument had to be created to accomodate the lowest notes – the *ránāt thūm*. Bamboo sticks with rounded ends are used to play these instruments, and those used on the *ránāt thūm* are padded to subdue the sound.

The gong is a very popular instrument in Thailand and was once used to signal daybreak. Thai gongs are given different names according to their size – they vary from 30 to 80 centimetres in diameter – and to their sonority. The one shown here (Pl. 41) is known as a *kháwng māyng*. It consists of a simple metal disc about one centimetre thick, with a protuberance at the centre and a handle at the top by which it may be hung up. The gong was beaten with a wooden cylinder that was sometimes padded at the end. There are, of course, many other kinds of gongs, some of them ornamented with characteristically Thai gilt motifs – letters and figures to which a magical significance is ascribed, highly stylized scrollwork and other designs.

Closely linked with music and dancing, the traditional theatre plays an important part in the life of the Thais. Through it is expressed the whole complexity of a philosophy and a way of life. There are two kinds of drama in Thailand: the *khon* theatre is a kind of masked pantomime and the *lakhon* is a form of epic entertainment resembling an opera-ballet.

An astonishing variety of masks are worn by the actors, and each mask corresponds in shape and colour to a precise character. There are masks for heroes, masks for the gods (Śiva, Vishnu and Brahmā), masks for monkeys, for the sea ogress and for demons, more than 100 of which have been listed. The iconographical criteria of the *khon,* which were laid down by the old masters, serve as identification devices, as do the arms and accessories that are always clearly differentiated. The audience must pay great attention to all these details if they wish to avoid confusion between the many characters. Most of these masks are made of moulded papier mâché. The surface is finely sandpapered, painted and coated with lacquer, and the craftsman then applies the colours. He adheres strictly to the code of symbols. In the present form of *khon,* only monkeys and other animals wear masks; people and gods are no longer required to do so. This development is regarded by some as a regrettable departure from tradition.

The *khon* theatre presents scenes from the *Rāmakien,* the Thai version of that very old Indian epic, the *Rāmāyana.* Amidst a part-magical, part-religious atmosphere, the story of the fight between Good and Evil is told, and the virtues of the warrior-hero are exalted as he overcomes Thotsakan and his terrible demons with his own army of monkeys, who are benef-icent creatures. It is impossible for the actors to speak, since they are wearing masks, so the text is spoken – or rather chanted – by a narrator, either in verse or in rhythmic prose. All the movements have been carefully worked out, sometimes over a period of a whole year, to fit in with this rhythm; nevertheless, they still retain all the freedom and grace of dancing. The physical effort demanded is much greater than one would believe at first sight, and the acrobatic routines require strict training. Every inclination of the head or upper part of the body, every movement of the fingers suggests an action or an emotion. The mime is accompanied by an orchestra of five instruments and a choir. The *khon,* therefore, is not just a simple entertain-ment but a full theatrical production, containing several different forms of artistic expression.

The *lakhon* is another very old form of Siamese theatre, comprising gracious movements rather than a show of virile strength. It is a kind of opera-ballet in which the actors play unmasked. Again they are accompanied by an orchestra and a choir, and the rhythm of the chanting and the music is emphasized more by hand and arm movements than by the movement of the lower limbs. The actors themselves do not sing, but they sometimes exchange snatches of dialogue.

In addition to this choreographic form of theatre there exists another kind of entertainment, similar to farce, that might be termed 'Siamese folk opera'. The *likay* is aimed above all at a rural public, and it always attracts a large audience, who enjoy the often improvised songs and dances and the bold jokes that are told in an extremely colourful dialect. The entertainment is usually based on some well-known folk-tale that is constantly being adapted according to the whim of the actors. No fair, no pagoda festival, no village celebration ever takes place without a performance of the *likay.* Today, extracts are often presented on radio and television, and the Thais never grow tired of them.

The shadow-theatre or *nang* is yet another very old form of Siamese dramatic art. The wonderful puppets, which are cut out of leather and projec-ted on to a canvas screen as silhouettes, have for centuries given pleasure to the Thais, who are so taken with the epic parts of the *Rāmāyana.* Today's westerns may have demythified all the beautiful old legends, but it is interesting to note that the Siamese have given their cinema the same name as the shadow-theatre – *nang* (which means leather). The *nang* may have come from India by way of Java. No one in fact knows its exact origin, although it is certain that it was already in existence at the time of Ayuthya and perhaps even as early as Sukhothai and that it constituted an important part of the entertainments that took place during official ceremonies. For the Thai people these leather figures are not merely puppets, they represent supernatural beings. As R. Nicolas writes in the *Journal of the Siam Society* (1927): 'The craftsman seeks perfection even in those details that are not essential.'

Before starting work the craftsman has to perform certain rites: he must clothe himself in white, make offerings of betel, areca nuts, coins hung on candles ... and even a calf's head! Having accomplished these rites he chooses the skin from which he will cut out the figures, buffalo or bull hide for the least important, the skin of a cow that died during pregnancy for the gods armed with bows and arrows, and bear or tiger skin for the ascetics. Certain parts are then coloured with plant or mineral extracts. Tree bark or *fang* for example produces red, and copper sulphate with lemon juice added gives blue. Convention requires that Vishnu and Rāma be painted green, Hanumān the monkey (son of the wind god) must be completely white and the Vice-King Sugriva red. The colours are purely symbolic, because theoretically the puppets are seen only as silhouettes projected on a screen. This art contains all the subtlety of Thai painting. 'The skill with which the Thai craftsmen have overcome all the difficulties,' writes Jean Boisselier in *Thai Painting*, 'is the result of a very long tradition, but it is still more due to an innate feeling for balance and artistic expression.' The *nang* is sometimes combined with the *khon* to provide variety in the acting and to avoid monotony. This more lively spectacle, however, loses in aesthetic beauty what it gains in movement.

It is not only through these theatrical creations, rites and entertainments that the Thais express their inborn love of beauty and harmony but at every moment of their daily lives. Their everyday gestures are full of charm and dignity: they greet each other by placing the hands palm against palm, with the fingers extended like a lotus-bud and the head slightly bowed; they offer a present with gracefully extended hands and sit on a cushion with elegantly folded legs. On all occasions their attitude is easy and relaxed. These gestures, so different from the strict ceremony of the Japanese, were established long ago by Buddhist tradition to which the people have remained faithful.

Thailand, the crossroads of the Asian civilizations, has been able to preserve its own way of life, despite the influences of India, China, Cambodia, Burma, Java and Sri Lanka. Let us hope that its genuine and vital culture will be able to resist industrialization and Western influence. It would help if a large museum of folk art were one day to open in Bangkok, and also if the Thai people (whose name means 'free men'), not content with preserving the nostalgia for objects that belonged to the past, would create new ones, just as interesting in their way as the old. The objects shown here — whether a kite, gliding in the sky, the movement of a dancer, a musical instrument or just a simple fish basket — are beautiful because they are well-suited to their different functions. As Louis Sullivan, the famous American architect and designer, said in 1896: 'The rule is that the object should always be suited to its function.'

Jean-Michel Beurdeley

3

4

5

6

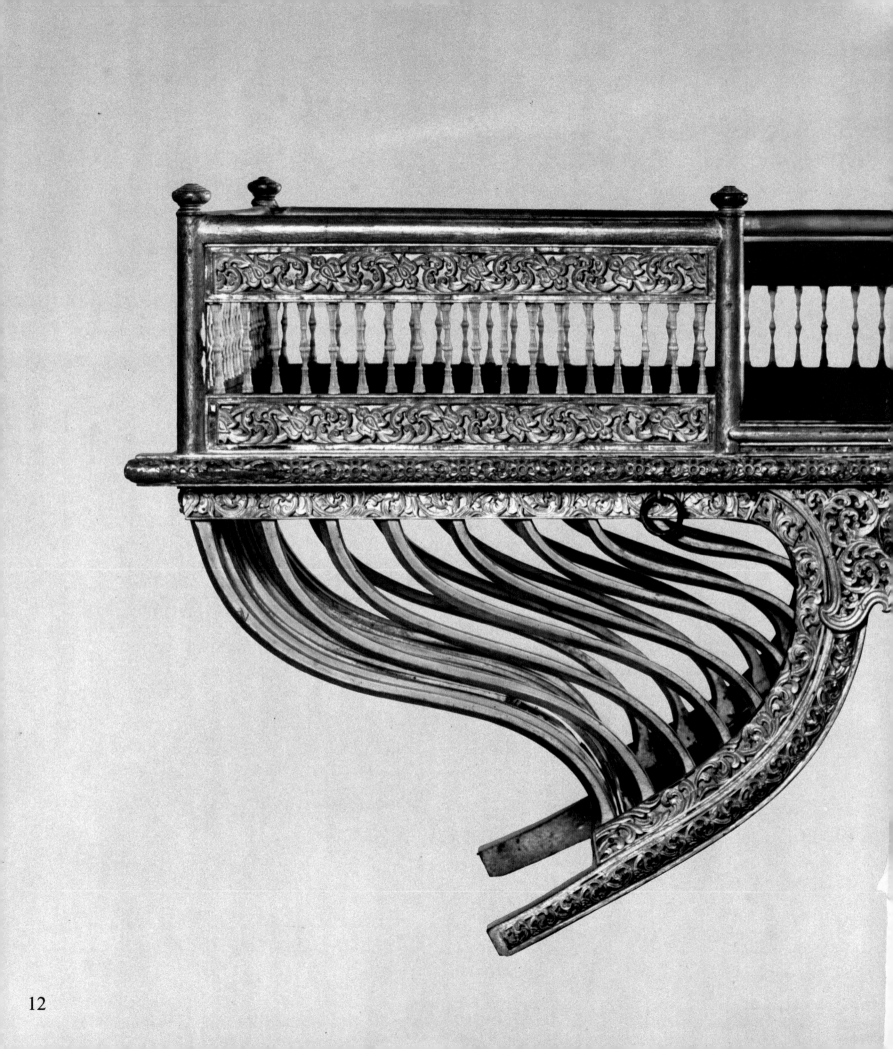

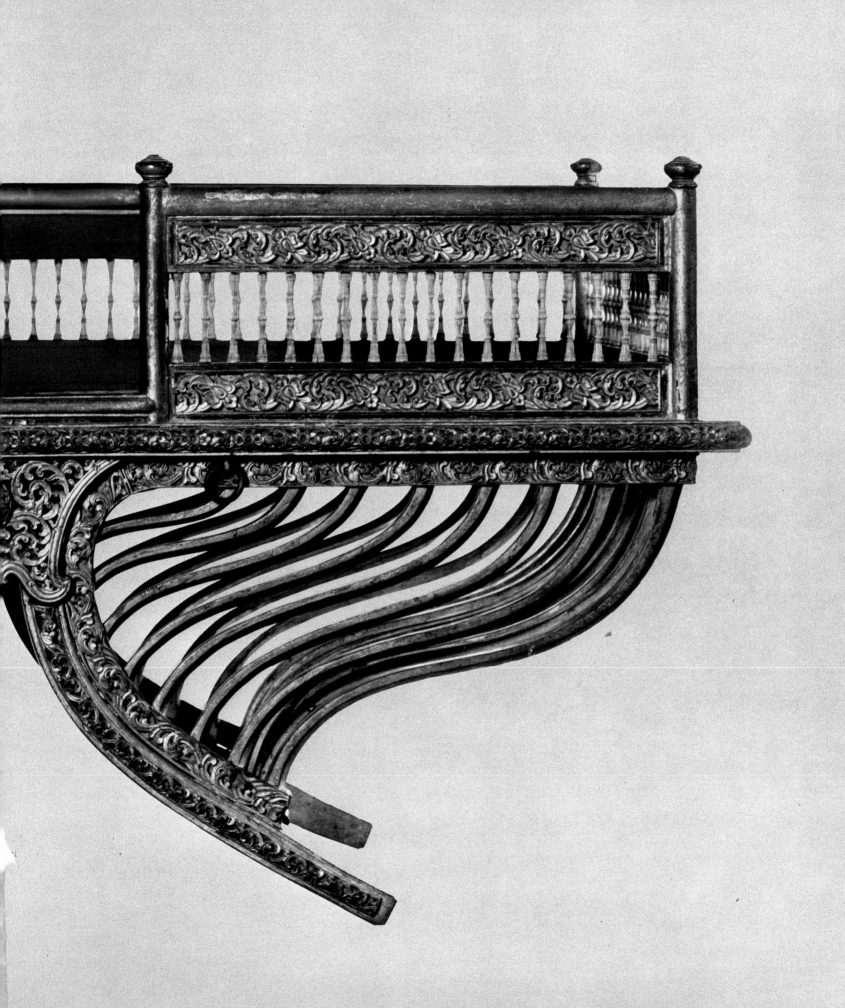

13

14

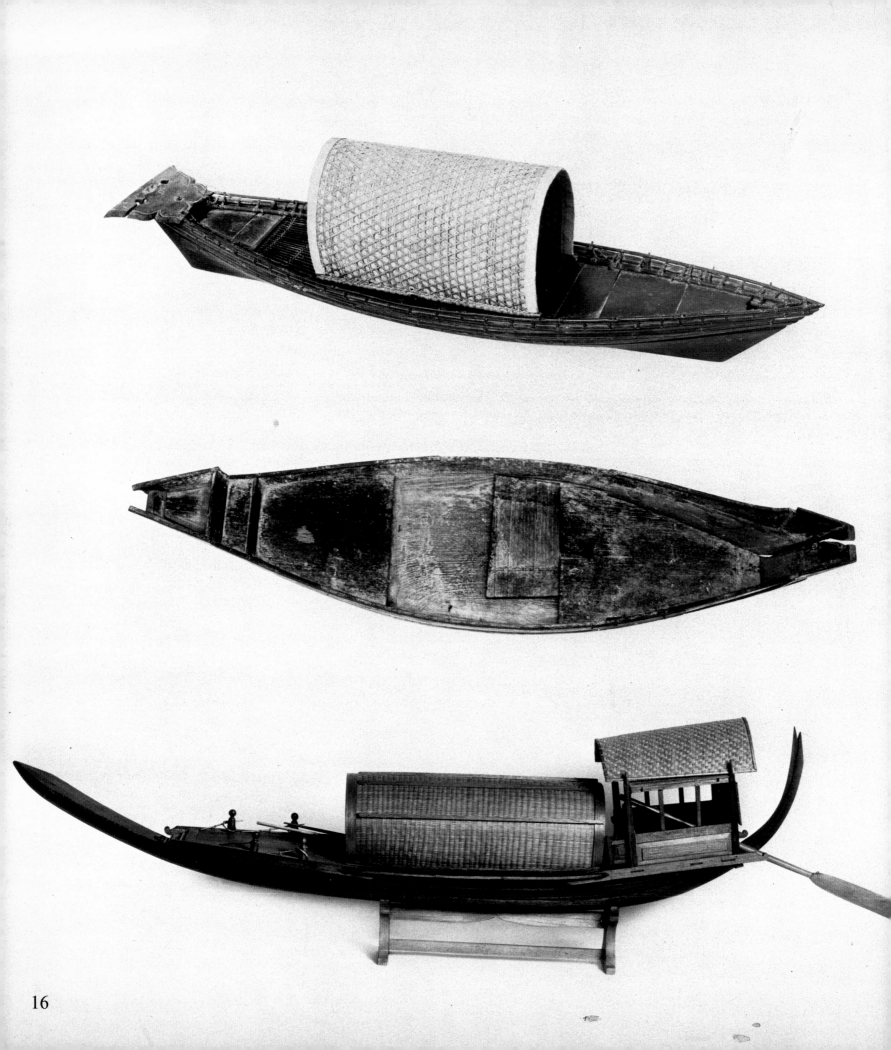

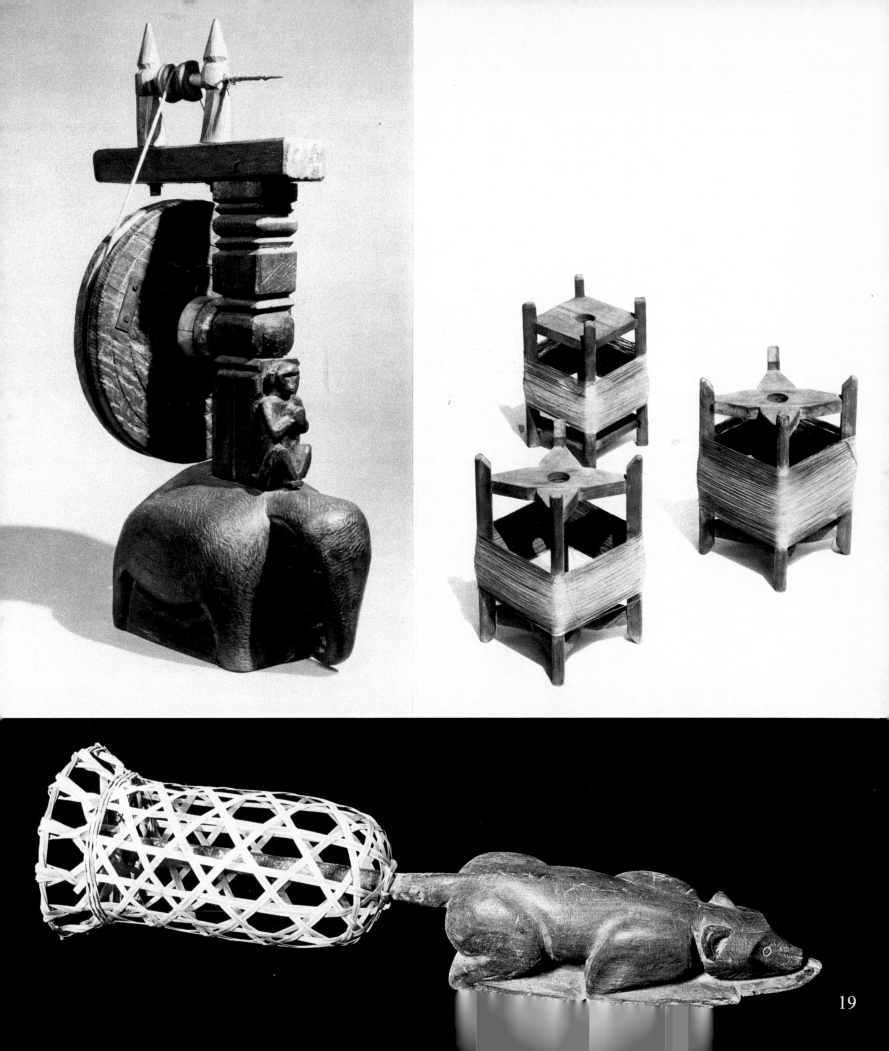

19

32

35

36

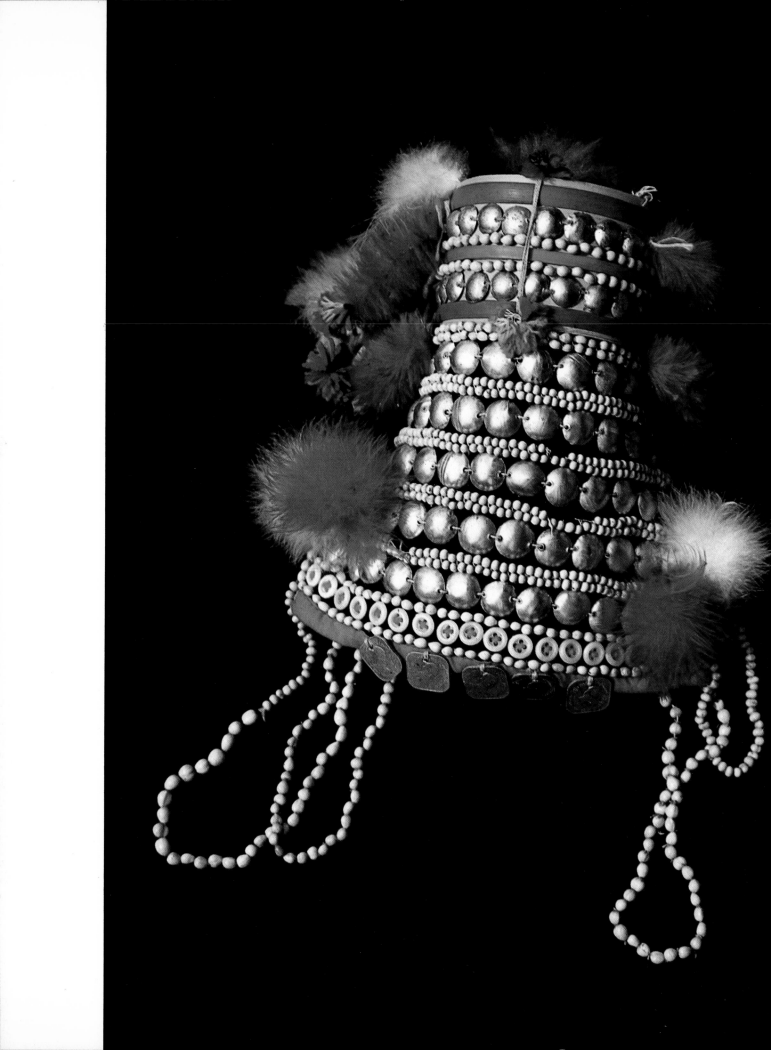

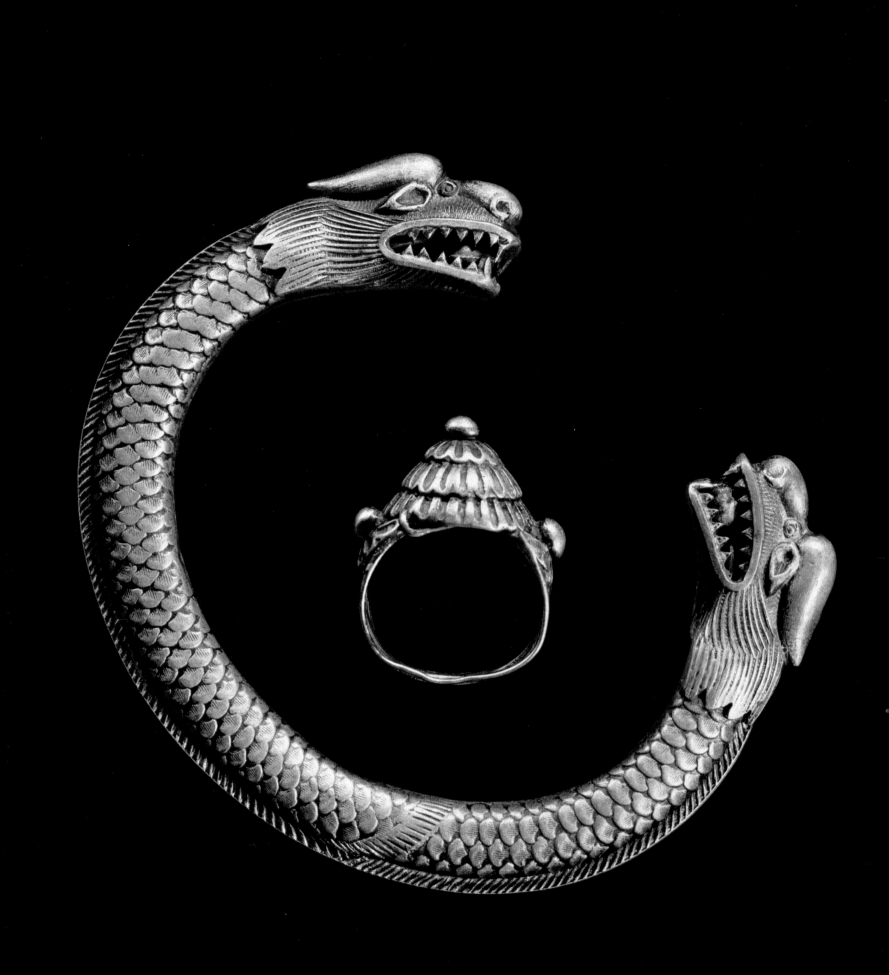

39

43

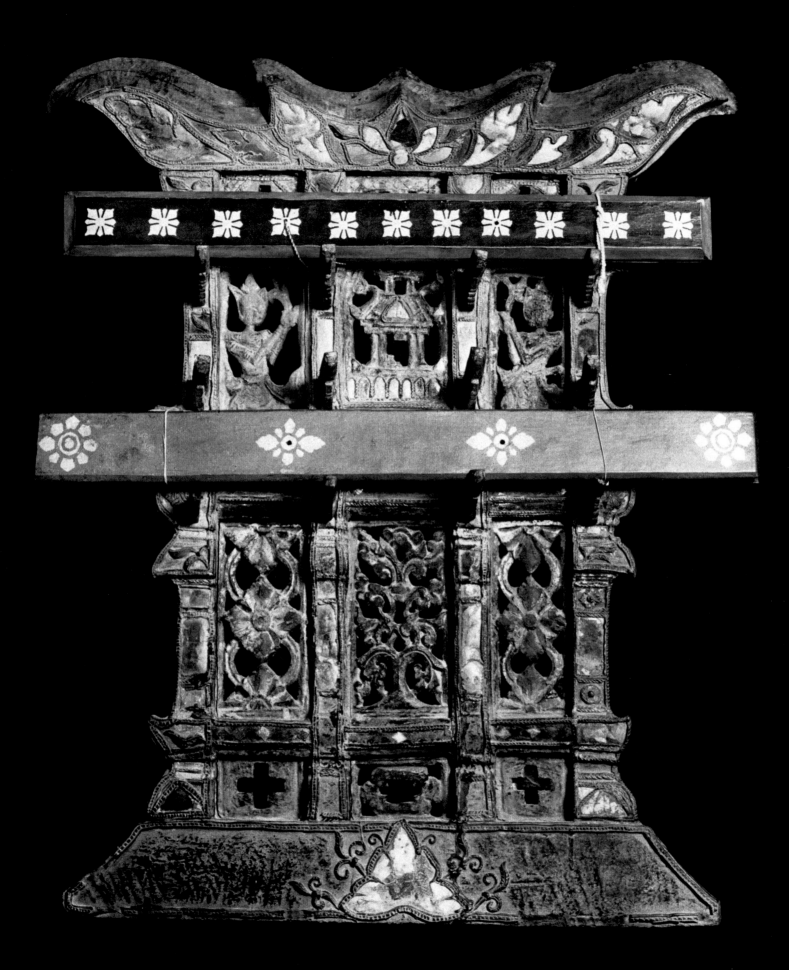

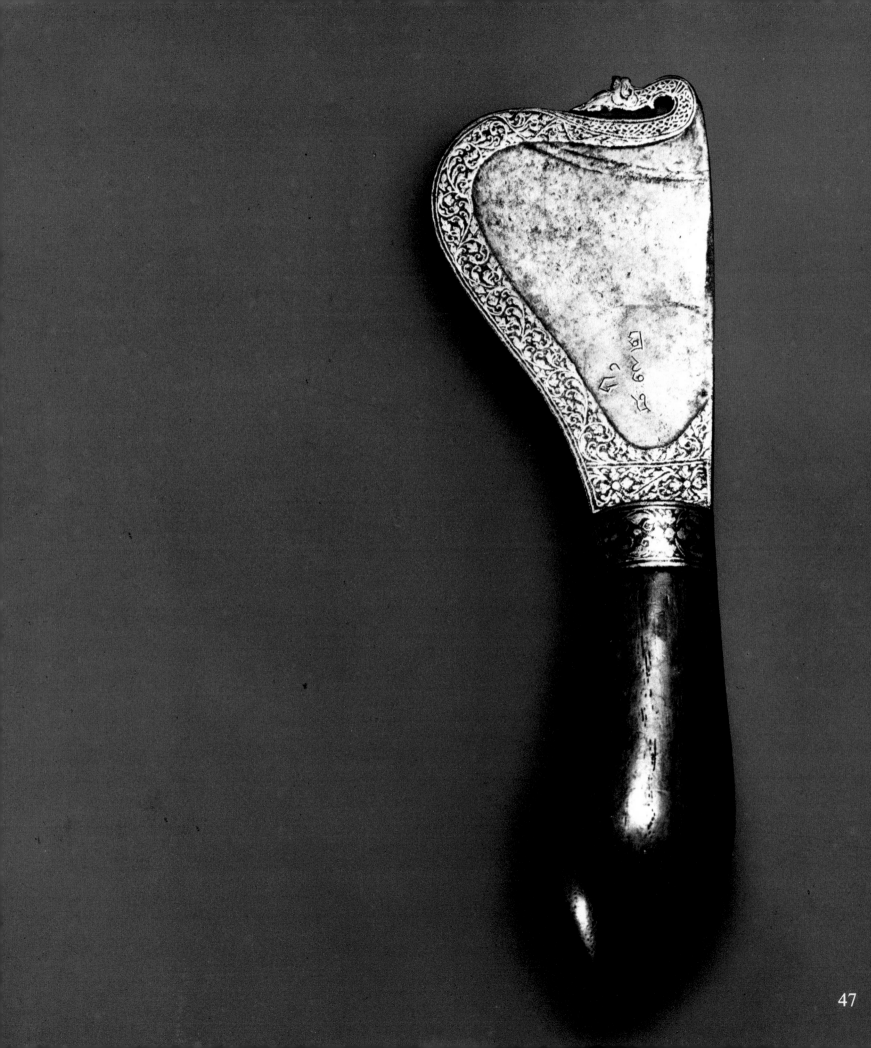

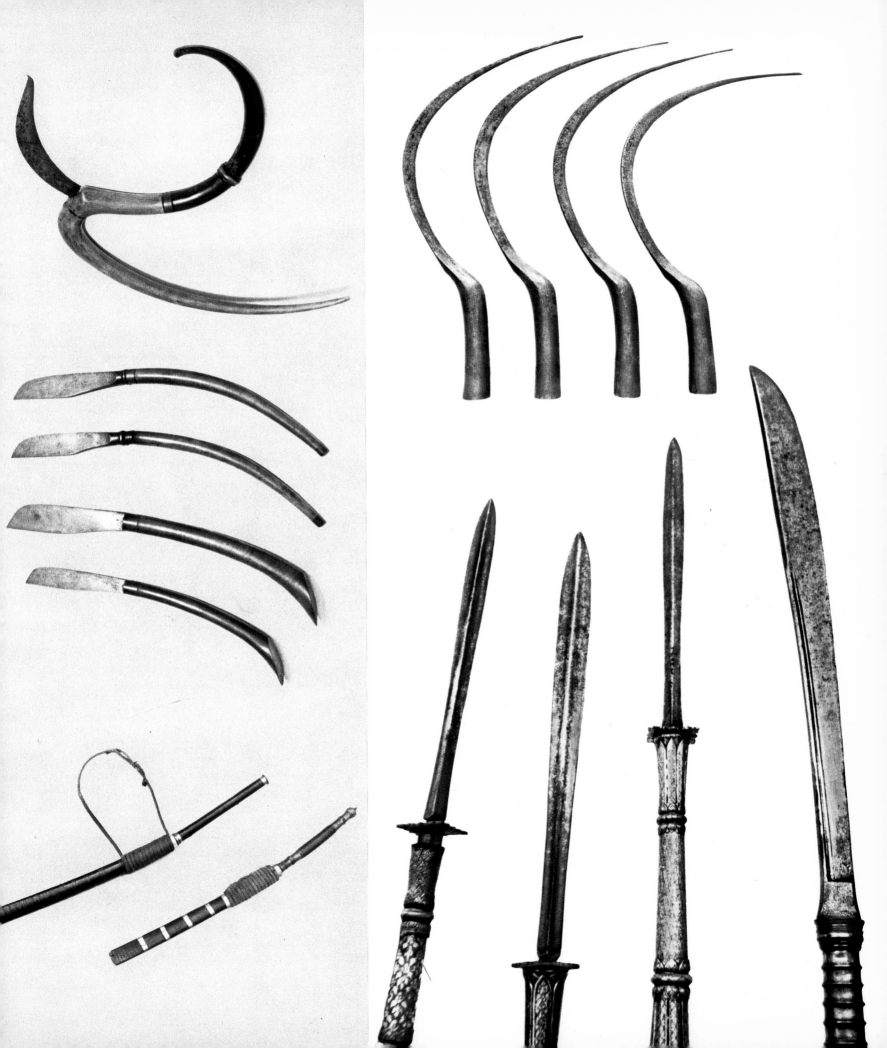

64

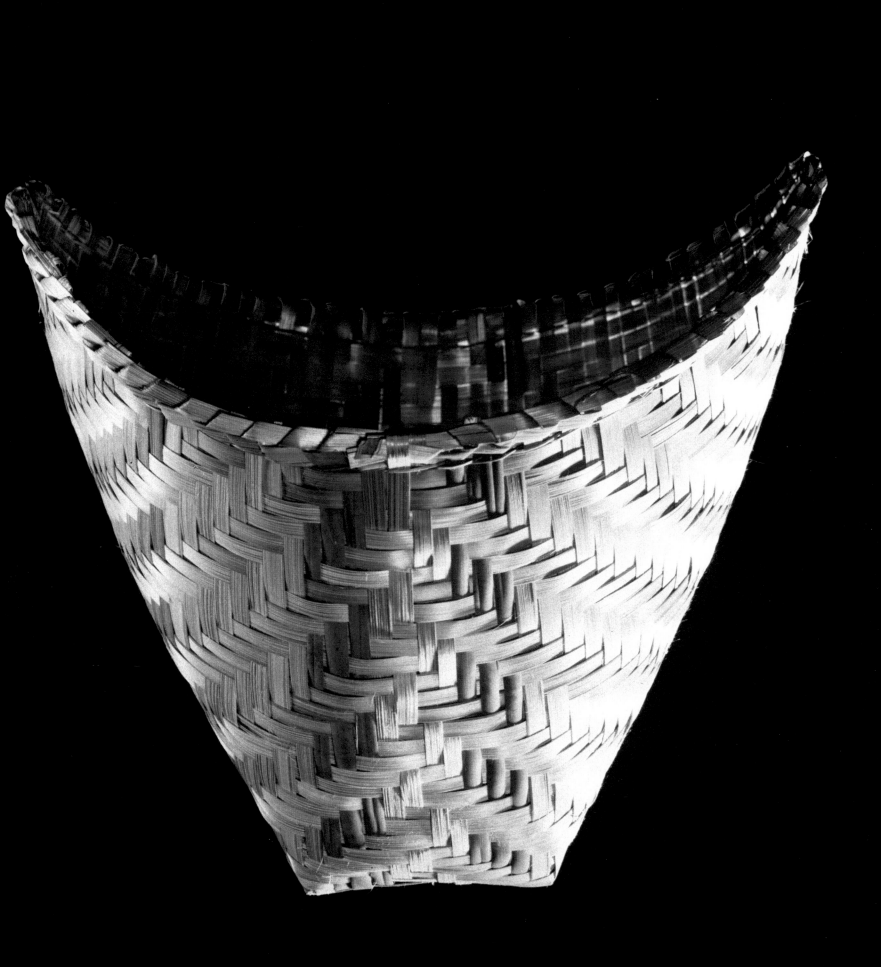

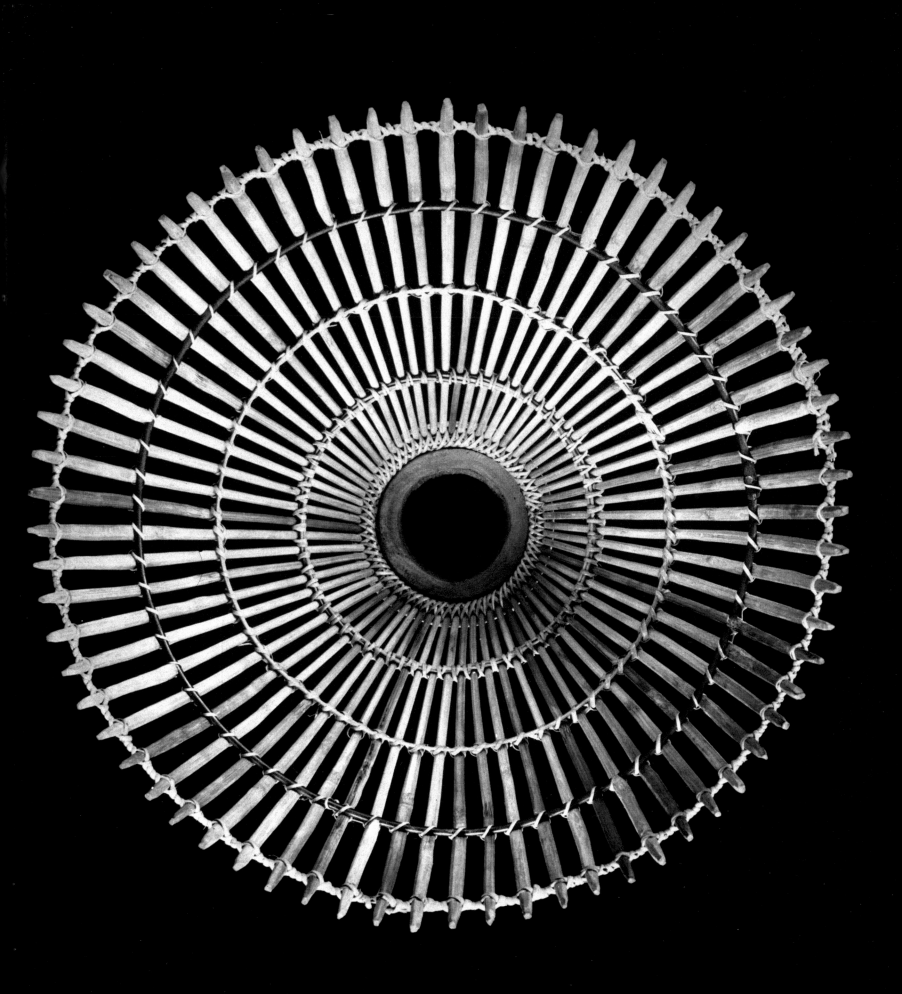

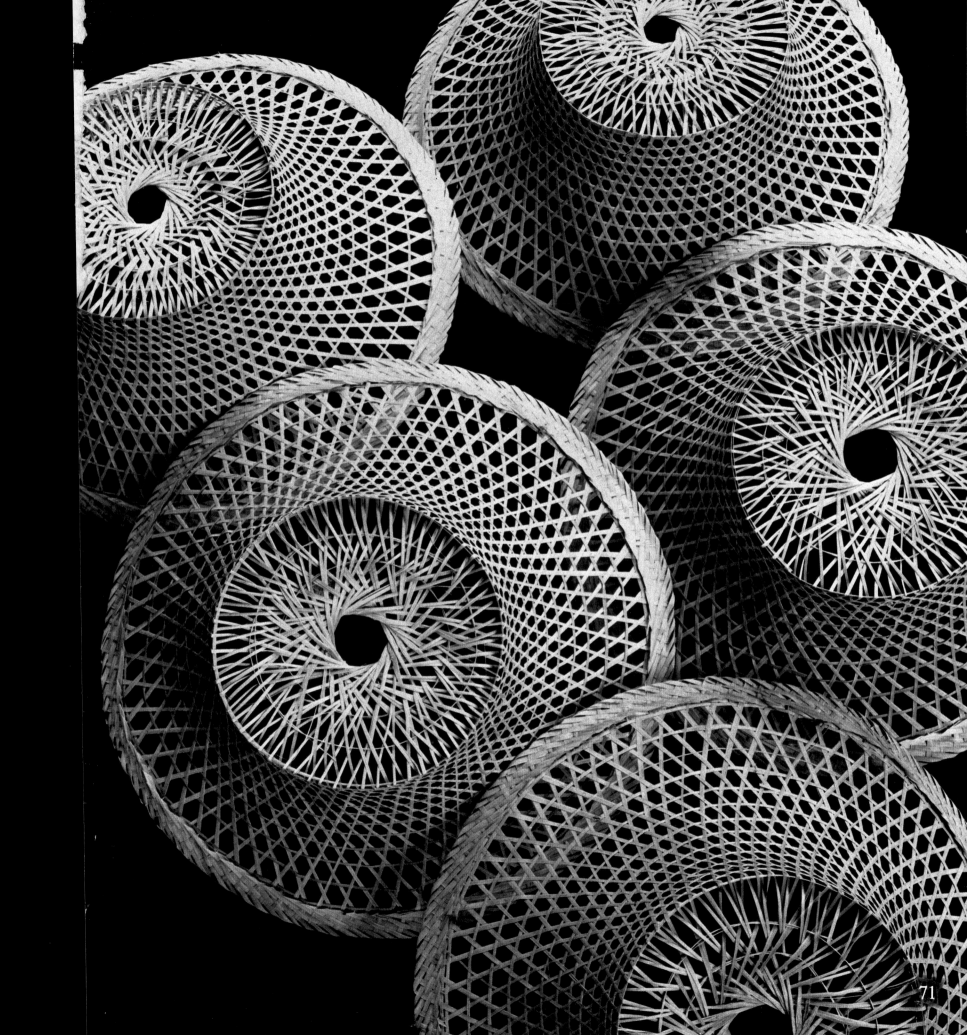

71

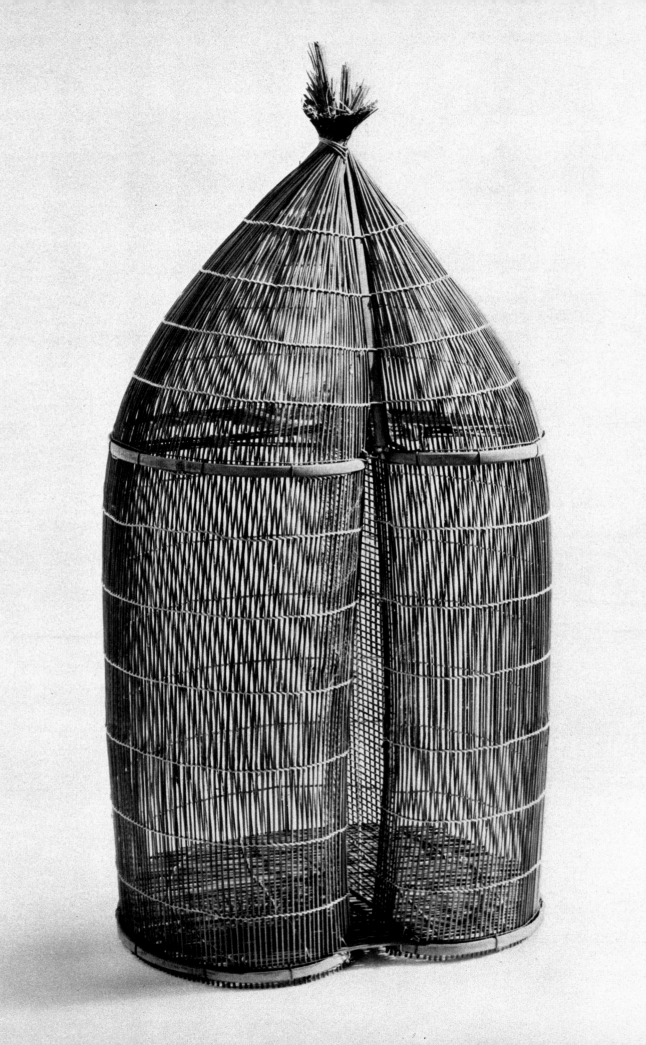

81

83

84

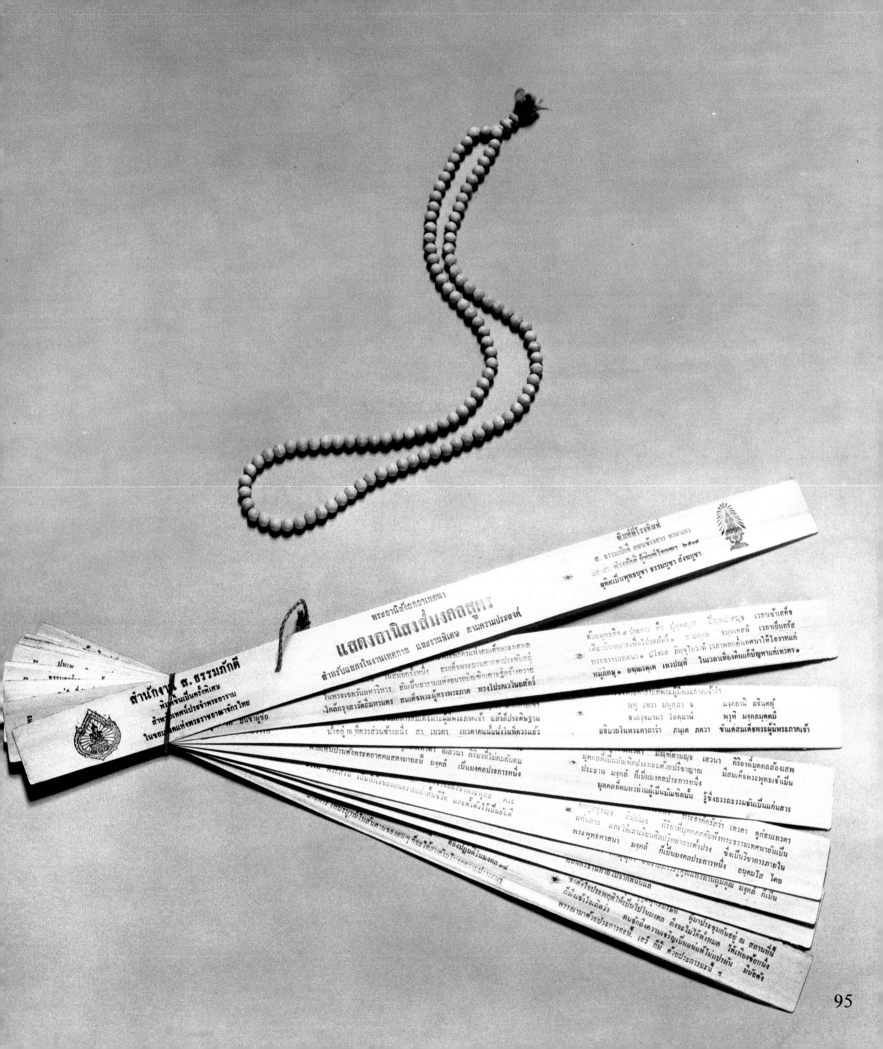

96

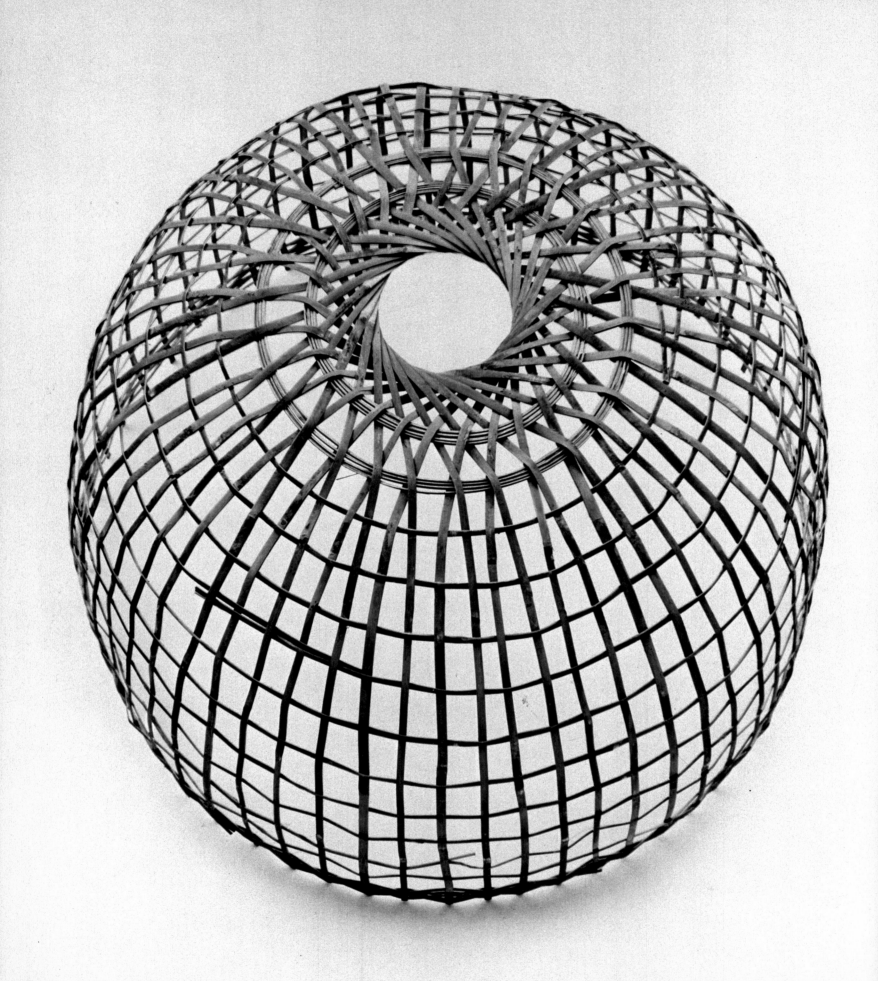

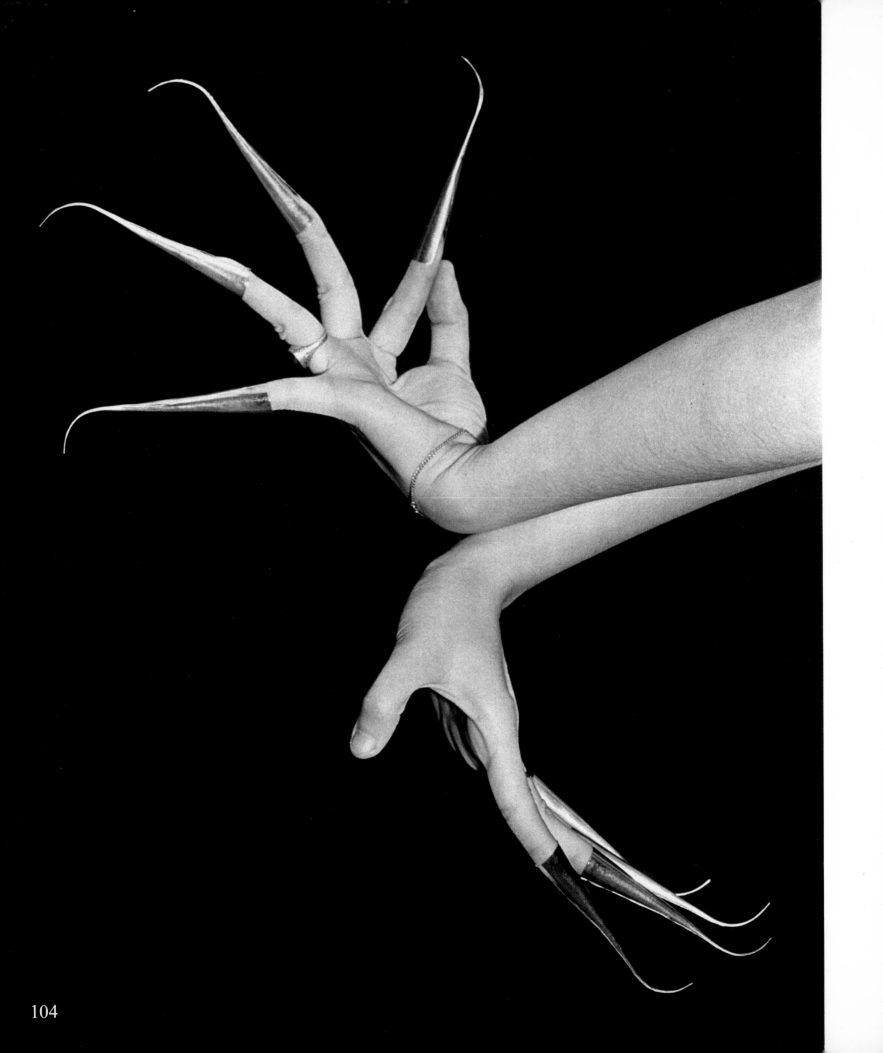

104

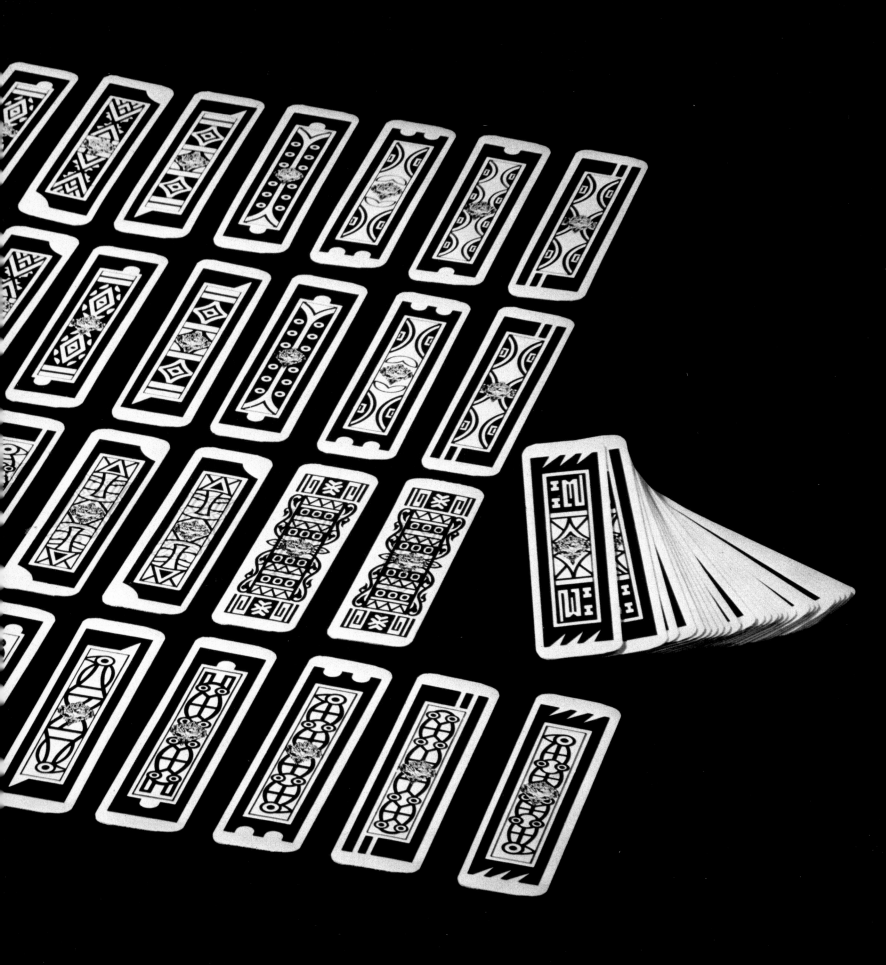

๑	๒	๓	๔	๕	๖	๗	จร
๑	๔	๖	๗	๕	๓	๗	ทักกะทิน
๑๒	๑๑	๗	๓	๖	๕	๗	ยมมะขัน
๔	๖	๑	๓	๕	๗	๑	ทระทึก
๑	๒	๑๔	๗	๕	๖	๓	อักคะนิโรด
๑๒	๑๑	๑๐	๗	๘	๗	๖	มฤตยู
๕	๒	๑๐	๗	๑	๗	๘	ทินะสูน
๘	๓	๗	๒	๔	๑	๕	อำมฤกะโชก
๑๑	๕	๑๕	๑๐	๗	๑๐	๘	สิทธิโชก
๑๘	๑๒	๑๓	๘	๗	๑๐	๑๕	มหาสิทธิโชก
๘	๓	๑๑	๑๐	๖	๑๐	๑๑	ไชยโชก
๖	๓	๘	๖	๑๐	๑๑	๘	ราศโชก

109

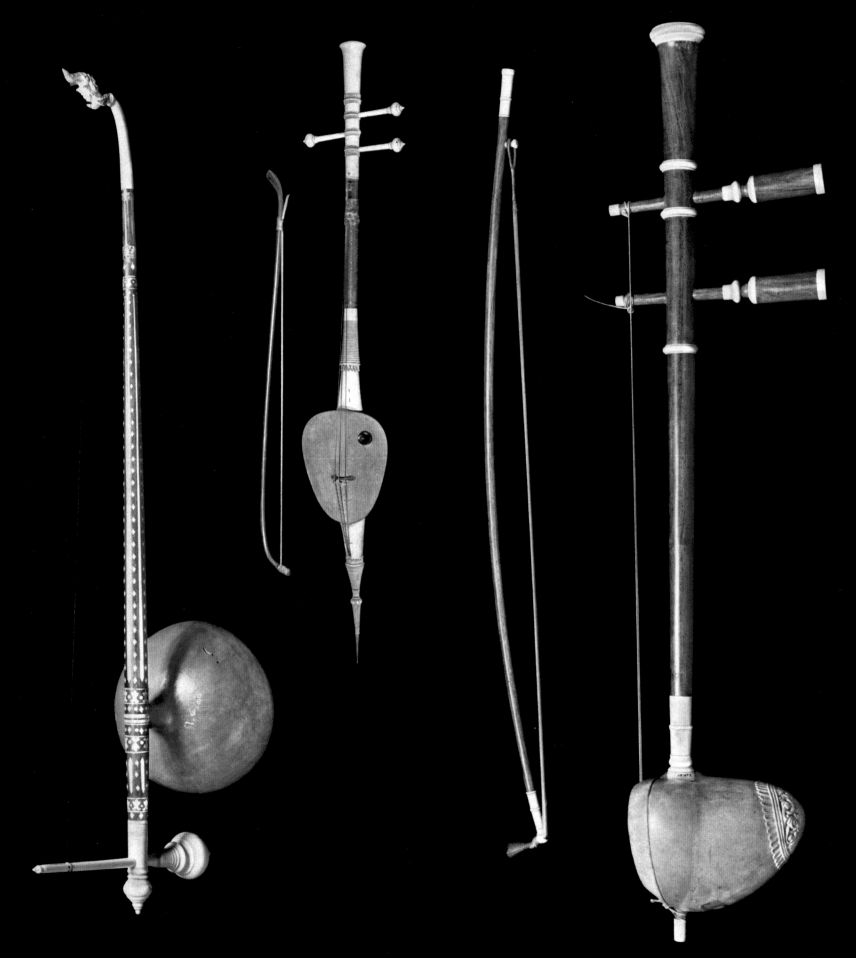

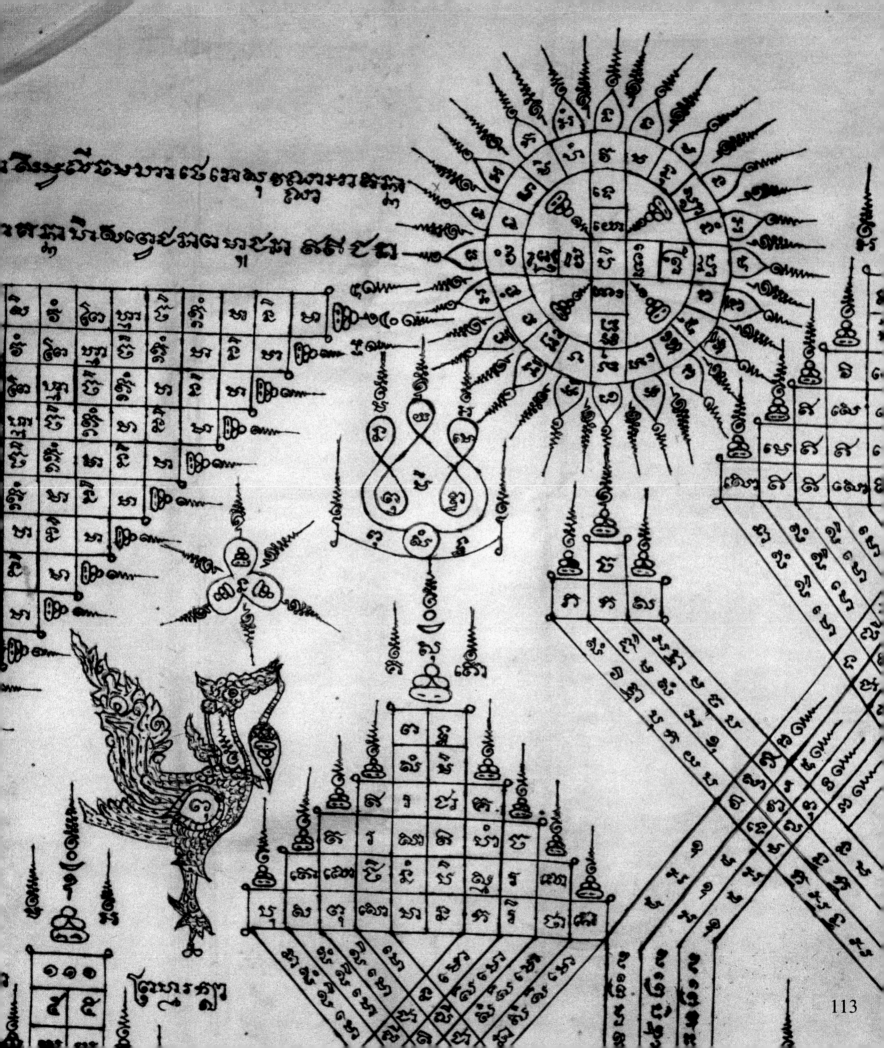

113

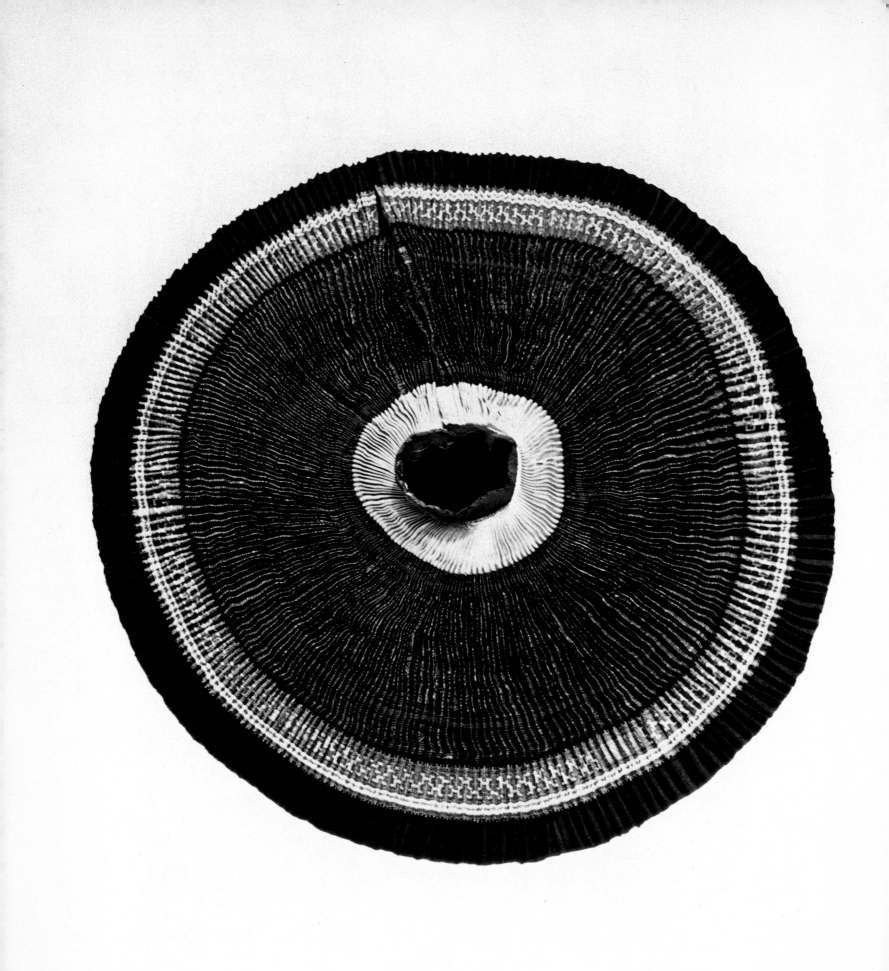

Captions for the Plates

1 Offering presented at Brahman ceremonies. Flower arrangement composed of banana-palm leaves, bamboo flowers and cooked rice. The bowl is nineteenth-century porcelain.

2 Floral decoration on a pedestal, composed of candles, incense sticks and a garland. Offering presented by the future Buddhist priest during the ordination ceremony.

3 Mobile of threaded flowers, representing a stylized crocodile.

4 Flower decoration placed at the tips of garlands.

5 Shrub shaped in the traditional Thai manner.
Suan Pakkad Palace, Bangkok.

6 Pediment of a rural house. North Thailand.

7 Roof of a wooden house with a projecting acroterium in the shape of a stylized *nāga*.
Saithong Shop, Chiang Mai.

8 Detail of a carved wooden panel from a pagoda, showing stylized fruit and plant motifs. North Thailand.

9 Tile roof with forward projections, topped by two *chofās* or 'heavenly bouquets'.
Buddhaisawan Chapel, Bangkok.

10 North Thai architecture. Balustrade and end of a carved wooden beam.
The Siam Society, Bangkok.

11 Plaited bamboo.

12, 13 Carved wooden palankeen carried by elephants. North Thailand.
Chiang Mai Museum.

14 Model wooden wagon with a wickerwork cover and model wooden carts. These carts are usually drawn by two buffalo.

15 Carved wooden carriage with a plaited wickerwork hood, remarkable for its elegant shape and fine ornamentation. North-east Thailand.
National Museum, Bangkok.
Below: carved wooden axle.

16 Three model boats made of wood and wickerwork.

17 Distaffs ornamented with mythical animals. North-east Thailand. Elephant Shop, Bangkok.

18 Large spinning-wheel constructed from a spindle fixed to a carved wooden horizontal support, decorated with floral motifs and an elephant.
James Thompson, Bangkok.

19 Spinning-wheel on a stand in the shape of a stylized elephant.
Square bobbins for unwinding the skeins.
Roller for holding a skein and unwinding the thread. The recumbent form of an animal provides the horizontal axis.

20 Drum known as a *thaphon* (literally, 'bound chest'). It is shaped from a single block of teak and the two ends, made of hide, are secured by the thongs covering the drum. The elaborately decorated stand is of black lacquered wood, inlaid with mother-of-pearl.

21 Barrel-shaped drums shaped from a single block of wood. The ends are made of hide, decorated with a circle and a ring painted in plant extracts. These drums were used in pairs, starting in the reign of Rāma II (1809–24).

22 Wind instrument made from two bamboo canes and a polished coconut.

23 Bamboo *angklung* that musicians shake to accompany their songs. This instrument probably originated in Indonesia.

24 Three ladles on a stand, made from coconut halves. The handles are of carved wood.

25 Bamboo receptacle for kitchen utensils.

26 Three coconut graters in the shape of stylized hares, each carved from a single piece of wood. The muzzle is prolonged to form an iron grater with a serrated edge. The user squats, with one foot on the animal's back and half a coconut in his hands. The flesh of the coconut is scraped off and gathered in the container.
The hare is a popular animal in Thailand and the sign of one of the years in the Jovian cycle.
Elephant Shop, Bangkok.

27 Hollowed-out wooden dishes used for preparing foods.
North Thailand.
Saithong Shop, Chiang Mai.

28 Figures from the *nang* or shadow-theatre, cut in a round piece of leather. They represent Hanumān and Supannamacha.

29 Cut-out leather figure from the *nang* or shadow-theatre, representing a flying divinity blowing into a shell.

30 Food container. The conical lid is made of wood inlaid with mother-of-pearl.
Suan Pakkad Palace, Bangkok.

31 *Left:* wickerwork bowl, black and red lacquer, with a medallion at the centre. North Thailand.
Chiang Mai Museum.
Wood and wickerwork box with several tiers; red and black lacquer decorated with leaves. North Thailand.
Right: three round red lacquer dishes with openwork at the centre, used as tables for offerings. North Thailand.
Chiang Mai Museum.

32 Two trays for offerings:
Above: in the shape of a lotus-blossom, made of lacquered wood, inlaid with mother-of-pearl.
National Museum, Bangkok.
Centre: black lacquered wood, inlaid with mother-of-pearl.
Suan Pakkad Palace, Bangkok.
Below: ránāt ayk of black lacquered wood inlaid with mother-of-pearl. This boat-shaped percussion instrument resembles a xylophone and has twenty-one keys.
Fine Arts Department, University of Bangkok.

33 Black and red lacquer table made of wood and wickerwork, sometimes used to hold offerings.
Chiang Mai Museum.

34 Offerings made by the congregation at the ordination ceremony of Buddhist priests. Candles and incense sticks are presented on a lacquer tray inlaid with mother-of-pearl.
National Museum, Bangkok.

35 Lottery pieces with Thai characters. Carved wood, set off with gold.
National Museum, Bangkok.

36 Necklace of beaten metal alloy with a high silver content, worn by mountain dwellers.

37 Cylindrical head-dress widening out at the bottom, decorated at the sides with pompoms and metal pieces.
North Thailand, Akha tribe.

38 Silver bracelet with dragon heads at each end. In the centre, a ring. North Thailand.

39 Small girl's loin-cloth.
Silver receptacle with engraved motifs. Design probably of Burmese influence.
Necklaces of beaten metal alloy with a high silver content and a bird's head at each end.

40 Bronze bell in a wooden frame. This type of bell used to be hung around the necks of elephants. North Thailand.
Chiang Mai Museum.

41 *Kháwng māyng,* a small gong with a carved wooden grasp, used at ceremonies.
Percussion instrument known as a *wong lek* gong, meaning a 'little circle of gongs'. It consists of eighteen gongs of different sizes supported by a raffia and ivory frame. The musician sits in the centre.
Fine Arts Department, University of Bangkok.

42 Bronze drum. The top is decorated with geometric designs consisting of circles with a star at the centre. These 'rain drums' are often decorated with frogs.
Suan Pakkad Palace, Bangkok.

43 *Ton* – a china percussion instrument used for accompanying songs and dances, like the *rām wong*. These used to be made in China for the Thai market.
National Museum, Bangkok.

44 Lacquered wooden stand for a holy book. The decoration shows strong Burmese influence.

45 Metal alms bowl covered with a net and having a shoulder-strap. The Buddhist priests use them every day to collect food offerings.

46 Knives with ivory or wooden handles, sometimes used for cutting areca nuts.
National Museum, Bangkok.

47 Areca-nut knife with a wooden handle and a gold edge inlaid with niello.

48 Hammer-wrought Chinese scissors of iron, used in Thailand since the Ming period (1368–1644).

49 *Left:* sickle with Z-shaped handle. East Thailand.
Bill-hook.
Sabres.
Right: hammer-wrought sickles of iron.
Lance-heads.
National Museum, Bangkok.

50 Libation conch set in gold on a stand in the shape of a lotus flower.
Suan Pakkad Palace, Bangkok.

51 Upper part of the balustrade of the *chedi* of Wat Pra That Lampang Luang.

52 Terracotta cooking pots. The oval bellies and curved necks date back to the Ayuthya period (fourteenth–eighteenth centuries).

53 Food container. The unobtrusive form sets off the restrained beige enamel decoration.

54 Stoneware jar, enamelled olive-green, for *nam pla*, a sauce made with small fermented fish.

55 Jars piled up in front of a potter's workshop. These brown stoneware jars with trails of greenish slip are well-balanced and functional.

56 Three terracotta water-pots with engraved designs. These are often placed at the entrances to houses in North Thailand.

57 Fragment of ceramic ware showing two fish, face to face: design of Chinese influence.
Sukhothai kiln, fourteenth century.

58 Decorative architectural pieces in enamelled terracotta.

59 Wickerwork receptacle with two bamboo floats. Used as a container for freshly caught fish.

60 Plaited bamboo receptacle used in Chinese steam-cooking and as a fish-holder at market stands.

61 Ball of plaited bamboo.

62 Detail of a plaited bamboo screen used in rural houses.

63 Bell-shaped wickerwork cones used to protect food from insects.

64 Inside of a hat with a round plaited crown. The central part expands to fit the head perfectly.

65 Conical bamboo steamer used for preparing sticky rice.

66 Detail of wickerwork.

67 Wickerwork basket with a square base on a cross-shaped stand.
North-east Thailand.

68, 69 Fish trap with a wide aperture at the base. The fisherman places it in shallow water, and the fish swims through the narrow opening at the top.

70, 71 Thai hat-frame shaped like a truncated cone, in the process of construction.

72 Inside of a basket with a square base.

73 Red lacquer wickerwork container for sticky rice, with wooden base. North Thailand.

74 Narrow-necked wickerwork basket used as a temporary container for freshly caught fish.

75 Large fish trap of plaited bamboo.

76 Plaited bamboo rake commonly used in China, Japan and the other South-east Asian countries.

77   Plaited bamboo basket with a square base. Great manual skill is required to make the base.

78, 79   Plaited bamboo bird-cages, exhibited outside a wickerwork shop. North Thailand.

80   Dove cage of rattan and bamboo. Doves are highly valued in Thailand.

81   Bottle rack of plaited wickerwork decorated with rabbits, birds and deer.

82   Well-bucket made of palm-leaves, with cross-piece handle. South Thailand.
Duangchit Shop, Chiang Mai.

83   Wooden yoke with two plaited wickerwork baskets — the most common method of transporting goods in Asia.
Square strainer with bamboo frame, used for preparing coconut milk.

84   *Above left:* rice container of plaited bamboo on a wooden base. North-east Thailand.
Right: bamboo bobbin.
Below: triangular landing-net of plaited bamboo.

85   Brushes of Chinese origin. The bamboo handles are joined together to achieve the desired thickness.

86   Laterite wall.

87   Brooms made of plant fibre with bamboo handles.

88, 89   Bamboo umbrella with waxed paper shade, stump-shaped hat made from latania leaves. Two familiar objects in Thai daily life.

90   Bamboo umbrella frames.
Chiang Mai region.

91   Waxed-paper umbrellas painted red and blue, drying in the sun before being decorated. North Thailand.

92   Coloured paper kite decorated with a serpent.

93   Small paper kites.

94   Fan in the shape of a stylized leaf, carried by the elders at religious ceremonies.

95   Objects used in the Buddhist service: wooden rosary and holy book. The Thai characters are printed on palm-leaves that are tied together.

96   Fan made of latania leaves with a wooden handle inlaid with mother-of-pearl. Buddhist priests carry these at festivals and ceremonies.

97   Paper banners used for decorating temples during religious ceremonies.

98   Plaited bamboo cage without base. The cage is placed directly on the ground. It houses different varieties of birds, but mainly fighting cocks.

99   Toy cock made of papier mâché.

100   *Nang Maëw* (Madam Cat), head-dress worn at ceremonies and also in the *Chai-Ya-Chet* theatre.

101   Head-dress worn by dancers, often when they are playing the horses of Rāma's chariot.
Bangkok School of Dance.

102   Demons' masks worn at the *khon* or classical dance theatre, which presents scenes from the *Rāmāyana*. On the right is the mask of Hanumān, King of the Monkeys; on the left is Thotsakan, King of the Demons.

103   Two head-dresses. On the left is a head-dress of the *Inao* theatre, in which the divine ancestor of Inao disguises himself as a peacock; on the right is a gilt papier mâché head-dress worn in performances of episodes of the *Rāmāyana*, when the demon Marich disguises himself as a stag.
Bangkok School of Dance.

104   Hand movement from the 'bird dance'. The fingers are lengthened by means of curved false finger nails that accentuate the hieratic elegance of the gesture.

105   High tiered tiara of gold lacquer, worn by female dancers.

106   Packs of playing cards.

107   *Saka:* a game played with ivory pawns and dice on a rectangular wooden board.
National Museum, Bangkok.

108, 109   Small ivory calendars used by astrologers and fortune-tellers to foretell auspicious dates.
National Museum, Bangkok.

110   *Left:* ivory official seal.
Peng Seng, Bangkok.
Right: fruit-shaped ivory boxes, containing ointment used

to coat the lips before chewing betel-leaves.
Suan Pakkad Palace, Bangkok.
Below: ivory tool used by masseurs, consisting of two protuberances on a carved base. This implement is more commonly made from two polished coconut halves.
Suan Pakkad Palace, Bangkok.

111   Detail of the base of a palankeen of finely carved ivory.
National Museum, Bangkok.

112   *From left to right:*
Phin nam tau – a string instrument made of wood and ivory, consisting of a sound-box in the shape of a half-gourd. The *phin,* of Indian influence, was probably introduced to the Indo-chinese peninsula before the migration of the Thais.
Cho sam sai – a string instrument resembling the Japanese *samisen* or the Chinese *san hsien,* made of ivory, wood and a half-coconut covered with hide.
Saw u – a string instrument made of wood and ivory. The sound-box is made of a half-coconut covered with hide. This instrument, probably of Chinese origin, appeared in Thailand at the end of the eighteenth century.
National Museum, Bangkok.

113   Tantric ink-drawing on cotton with Thai motifs and Khmer characters, which are often used in magical texts.

114   Embroidered cushions that are placed on matting.

115   Silk sarong material. North-east Thailand.
James Thompson, Bangkok.

116   Embroidered skirt worn by women of the Hmong (Meo) tribe in North Thailand.

117   Ikat fabric. Probably a very old traditional motif from the Dōng-sön civilization (500–200 B.C.). This type of fabric is found in Thailand, Bali and Sumatra.

118   Small packages made from banana-palm leaves, containing Siamese salami. North Thailand.

119   Dried fish.

120   Cut-out leather figure from the *nang* or shadow-theatre, representing a divinity playing the *cho sam sai.*

This book was printed in January, 1980.
Photosetting: Hertig+Co. S.A., Bienne
Photolithography in colour: Vaccari Zinco-Grafico,
Modena, Italy
Helioengraving, printing and binding: Heraclio Fournier
S.A., Vitoria, Spain
Design: Hans Hinz SWB and W. O. Buser
Editorial: Barbara Perroud-Benson
Production: Yves Buchheim

Printed in Spain